Apostle De Burney

CHRIST
Christ
CHRIST

"It Is Finished"

IT IS FINISHED

WHAT IS FINISHED?

cCopyright © 2023 Apostle De Burney

Apostle3477@gmail.com

ISBN: 978-1-7323254-8-7

All rights reserved. No part of this publication may be reproduced or transmitted in any form or by any means, mechanical or electronic, including photocopying or recording, or by any information storage and retrieval system, or transmitted by email without permission in writing from the publisher.

While all attempts have been made to verify the information provided in this publication, neither the author nor the publisher assumes any responsibility for errors, omissions, or contrary interpretations of the subject matter herein.

This book is for education purposes only. The views expressed are those of the author alone and should not be taken as expert instruction or commands. The reader is responsible for his or her own actions.

Adherence to all applicable laws and regulations, including international, federal, state, and local governing professional licensing, business practices, advertising, and all other aspects of doing business in the US, Canada, or any other jurisdiction is the sole responsibility of the purchaser or reader

Table of Contents

Introduction	7
Chapter 1 God Hates Sin	**11**
Breaking One Commandment Breaks Them All	13
Things God Considers An Abomination To Him Is Sin	14
All Our Righteousness are as Filthy Rags (as Sin)	24
All Have Sinned (*Sin is Our Problem*)	26
Chapter 2 If Sin Is Our Problem, What Gives Sin Its Power?	29
When Sin Is Conceived, It Gives Birth To Death	30
Sin Is From The Devil	31
Practices of Sinful Nature	34
No One Is Justified by The Law	36
Chapter 3 Christ Came To Destroy The Work Of Satan (SIN)	38
What Is The Work Of Satan?	38
Jesus Came To Take Away Our SINS	39
THE "BLOOD" Of *JESUS* Wipes Out "ALL" Sin	40

Chapter 4 What Gives Christ The Authority to Change God's Laws?   44

Jesus Is Our Compassionate High Priest   47

Christ Redeem us From the Curse   52

Chapter 5 What Has Changed With The Laws Through Our New High Priest, Christ?   54

Christ Came To Fulfill The Law   54

Christ Fulfilled Righteousness Of Law   57

Christ has set us Free From the Law of Sin and Death   58

Free Of The Guilt Of Sin And Granted Eternal Life   59

No Longer Bound by Sin   60

Chapter 6 Righteousness Completed For Us By God   62

Righteousness of God Apart From The Law   63

Many Would Be Made Righteous Through Christ   65

Grace Reign Through Righteousness Through Christ   66

Chapter 7 It Is Finished   69

Death in Adam or Life in Christ?   71

Christ Makes Us Right With God By Faith   74

Introduction

John 19:28-30(NIV): *Later, knowing that everything has now been Finished FOR US, so that Scripture would be fulfilled, Jesus said, "I am thirsty." A jar of wine vinegar was there, so they soaked a sponge in it, put the sponge on a stalk of the hyssop plant, and lifted it to Jesus' lips. When he had received the drink, Jesus said, **"IT IS FINISHED"** With that, he bowed his head and gave up his spirit.*

The Greek word Tetelestai, which is the last thing Jesus' said before dying on the cross, translates to *"It Is Finished"* in English. Tetelestai originates from the verb teleo, meaning "to **Complete**, to bring to an **End,** to **Accomplish.**" The word is essential because it signifies the successful end to a specific event. Meaning CHRIST has **ACCOMPLISHED** what GOD had sent him here to BRING TO an **END** Christ **COMPLETED** His Mission!!

Jesus completed this Mission by his Death and Resurrection on the Cross. The Finished Work of God. How did he achieve this work God sent him here to do? By destroying the work of Satan. Satan's work is he brought in Sin, which separated us from God. And the scripture says Christ came to destroy Satan's work **(1 John 3:8)**. He did this by sacrificing his Blood on the Cross, in which the scriptures state, *"The Blood of Jesus Wipes Out All Sin"* **(1 John 1:7)**—Thereby connecting us back to God.

For instance, you would use the word "Tetelestai" when you submit the final copy of your dissertation; you would use it when you embark on a journey and reach your destination; you would use it when you make the final payment on your new house; you would use it when you finish a tedious task. When you use this word, it is not merely to say, *"I survived."* You're also saying, *"I did exactly what I set out to do."*

But beyond the verb itself, the word Tetelestai is in a perfect tense in Greek. This is noteworthy because the perfect tense signifies an action that has results that continue into the present although completed in the past. It differs from the past tense, which views an event that happened in the past and says, *"This happened."* *The perfect tense helps you understand that "This happened, and it is still in effect presently."*

Jesus crying out *"It is finished,"* on the cross meant "It was finished in the past, it is utill finished in the present, and it will remain finished in the future."

The Bible tells us that Jesus Christ. He glorified God by finishing His work here on earth, which are words that comfort and inform us. Alongside destroying conditionalism and sacramentalism. Many in Christianity believe that he only made salvation possible, so anyone could come to him if they met certain conditions? If meeting these conditions was true? Thereby, he would be subsequently involved in the evils of decisional regeneration, sacramentalism, and other heresies in salvation.

Explained furthermore, many Christians believe that a large percentage of the people Jesus died for end up in hell, and anyone who makes heaven gets there solely through ththrough their own works, not by HIs finished work. Most of the religious world leaves Him quite unhappy now and for eternity, because He came so far short of accomplishing His desire. If His Intention was to give all mena access to salvation, why didn't He? If his intention was to give all men a second chance, why did he give life to so many He knew would reject Him?

Making any additions to the finished work of Jesus Christ destroys the gospel (Ga 2:21; 5:4; I Co 1:30-31). By the time the events of John 19:30 occurred, He had been without sleep for 33 hours, spent the last 12 being tortured, and the last 3 in darkness. He saw His Seed - the generation of children God had given Him by-election - and He saved them. In general terms, the death, resurrection, ascension, and coronation of Jesus Christ are all one event.

Christ paid the PRICE in full with His life; the work of salvation is now accomplished. That is the meaning of *"It is finished."* The debt - paid in full, He achieved the FULL results- he completed the Sacrifice. The verb is in perfect tense indicates that the death of Jesus was once and for all time. A sacrifice is sufficient to atone for the sins of every individual who has ever lived - past, present or future (1 John 1:7).

The completed sacrifice of Christ explains what theologians call the *"finished work"* of Jesus Christ, which is not just a mantra but a profound spiritual truth. With his death, Jesus accomplished work so exceptional, so total, so utterly complete that it could never be copied or repeated, not even by Jesus himself. *"It is finished."* There is no Plan B to save the human race. Plan A (the death of Christ) was PERFECT!!!!

Since the work of Christ DID ON THE CROSS IS FINISHED! Any attempt to add additions to His work on the cross is doomed to failure. As Christians, we believe that nobody can see the kingdom of God unless they are born again. No heights of morality however high, no level of reformation however great, no culture however pure, no baptism no matter how administered can take a sinner even one step closer to heaven; except they assume a new nature imparted from above. A new being implanted by the Holy Spirit through the Word of God is crucial to salvation, and only those saved by this means are the sons of God. Likewise, we believe that our redemption has been purchased solely by the blood of Jesus Christ our Lord, who was made to become sin and a curse for us, dying in our stead; and that no faith, no repentance, no remorse, no sincere efforts, no good resolutions, no obedience of the rules and regulations of any church, nor all the churches that have been in existence since the days of the Apostles can add to the value of the blood or to the perfection of the finished work of Jesus Christ in the slightest way

This statement is all-encompassing. It is impossible to make any addition to the merit of Christ's work on the cross. All such efforts are doomed to failure. In simpler terms, if Jesus paid it all, then you don't have to. If you attempt to pay for your salvation, then you don't believe he paid it all. There is no in-between; God is not asking you to buy salvation. God does not have a sale on salvation, nor is He asking you to "Dutch Treat" with you. And He's definitely not offering an installment plan on salvation. He is offering you salvation free of charge, without any hidden charges. Tetelestai means Jesus paid in full so that you wouldn't have to pay anything.

Chapter 1
God Hates Sin

Ever wondered why God hates sin? Quite simple. Sin is the direct opposite of God's nature. The psalmist explains God's hatred of sin: *"For You are not a God who takes pleasure in wickedness; no evil dwells with You"* (Psalm 5:4). God abhors sin because He is holy, and holiness is the most exalted of all His attributes (Isaiah 6:3; Revelation 6:8). God's holiness completely saturates His being. His holiness embodies His moral perfection and His total removal from blemishes of any kind (Psalm 89:35; 92:15; Romans 9:14).

In the Bible, we can see how God feels about sin. He looks toward sin with intense feelings of hostility, anger, disgust, and utter dislike. For instance, sin (corruption, evil) is depicted as decaying sores (Isaiah 1:6, NKJV), defiling filth (Titus 1:15; 2 Corinthians 7:1), darkness (1 John 1:6) a binding debt (Matthew 6:12-15), a heavy burden (Psalm 38:4), and a scarlet stain (Isaiah 1:18).

James 2:10-13 (NKJV): *"For whoever shall keep the whole law, and yet stumble in one point, he is guilty of all. For He who said, "Do not commit adultery," also said, "Do not murder." Now if you do not commit adultery, but you do murder, you have become a transgressor of the law.*

The Old Testament describes a sacrificial system that we cannot even begin to fathom. We often find Leviticus tedious to read because we lack an understanding of each sin's gravity. It is impossible to exaggerate the significance of the Old Testament. God takes sin very seriously as it separates us from God, and He devised the sacrificial system so that we as humans could get a glimpse of fellowship with Him. People who offered their animals as a sacrifice had their sins temporarily forgiven, therefore giving them a temporary fellowship with God, right up until they commit the next sin. Sacrifice was essential. Hebrews 9:22 says, *"And according to the law almost all things are purified (cleansed) with blood, and without shedding of blood there is no remission (forgiveness)."*

To give us an understanding of how seriously God took sin, He came down as Jesus Christ and offered Himself a sacrifice, the only lasting solution to our sin problem. It is impossible for anyone to keep all of the Laws that God had given, and coupled with religious leaders of the day adding more laws to prevent people from breaking the main laws, it was extremely difficult. The people's periodic and annual sacrifices showed how impossible it was to keep oneself from sin. From the beginning of creation, God knew all of this and knew that He would have to provide a permanent way for us to be reconciled to Him. John 14:6 says, *"Jesus said to him, 'I am the way, the truth, and the life. No one comes to the Father except through Me.'"* Through the death, burial, and resurrection of Jesus Christ, every sacrificial requirement of the Old Testament was met and exceeded.

The Bible recorded James explaining to people that it was impossible for them to earn righteousness. Just like it is today, people in Jesus' era were wont to justify themselves with statements like, "Well, at least I haven't murdered anyone." Or, "At least I'm not an addict." James explained that breaking just one of God's laws means you can't be called completely righteous. 1 Corinthians 1:30-31 says, *"But of Him you are in Christ Jesus, who became for us wisdom from God - and righteousness and sanctification and redemption - that, as it is written, 'He who glories, let him glory in the Lord."*

Jesus became our *"righteousness, sanctification,* and *redemption!"* If we have to brag, then we about Jesus. Romans 3:23 reminds us that *"All have sinned and fallen short of the glory of God."* Matthew 5:17 had even greater news where Jesus says, *"Do not think that I came to destroy the Law or the Prophets. I did not come to destroy but to fulfill."* He truly did pay it completely for our sake. If Jesus didn't pay it all, we would be nothing, and without Him, we would have nothing to offer God for our sins.

Breaking One Commandment Breaks Them All

James 2:10-11 [AMP]: *For whoever keeps the whole Law but stumbles in one point, he has become guilty of [breaking] all of it. For He who said, "Do not commit adultery," also said, "Do not murder." Now, if you do not commit adultery, but you murder, you have become guilty of transgressing the [entire] Law.*

James declared that to show favoritism to a wealthy person over a poor one is a sin. Such a person has failed to obey God's command to love others just as we love ourselves. By definition, we become lawbreakers.

James understands that it is human for us to dismiss our sin, but he's not going to let us off easily as he reveals that to commit the sin of favoritism and prejudice makes us equally as guilty as if we had set out to break every single command in the Law. This is not to say that all sins are similarly abominable; instead, it is that on God's legal sheet, even one sin is ruinous for those who will be judged according to the Old Testament Law. A person is either perfect or not. There is no middle ground. Stumbling once gives us the same result as if we had lived a life of deliberate disobedience.

From verse 10, James continues his thoughts on the eternal consequences of sin. Anyone who "stumbles" over a single command in God's Law is equally as imperfect, and therefore guilty, as one who systematically breaks all of the commands in His Law. They have both failed to keep the Law. They are both lawbreakers.

James drives the point home here. Which is worse between adultery and murder? Many think one is terribly worse than the other. However, James says that's not essential when it comes to our salvation. Committing either one of these offenses makes you a lawbreaker. Committing one sin and not that other sin is not a valid defense for the sins you commit.

In the 3rd chapter of Romans, Paul had a very similar thought but went a bit further by saying: *"Everyone is a lawbreaker. Everyone has sinned and, by definition, falls short of God's glory (Romans 3:23).* Because we all fall short of God's Glory; is the reason why we need God's forgiveness, why we need Him to judge us according to the goodness of Jesus and not our own. In the next verse, Paul continues his declaration that all have sinned and have fallen short of his glory. Paul declares, "We *are justified by his grace as a gift, through the redemption that is in Christ Jesus. (Romans 3:24)."*

Things God Considers An Abomination To Him Is Sin

Proverbs 6: 16-19 (AMP): *These six things the Lord hates; Indeed, seven are repulsive (it says an Abomination in [NKJV]) to Him: A proud look, a lying tongue, and hands that shed innocent blood, A heart that creates wicked plans, Feet that run swiftly to evil, A false witness who breathes out lies, and one who spreads discord among brothers.*

Proverbs 6 is a very sobering passage of Scripture. In verse 16: *"These six things the Lord hates: Indeed, seven are repulsive (it says an Abomination in [NKJV]) to Him."* Many people have often come across that verse but are usually taken aback when they confront it for the first time. Questions like "But doesn't the Bible say, 'God is love?" arise, and yes, the Bible says so. However, the Bible also explains some things that God hates, and below are seven of them.

We must understand that God's hatred and man's hatred are two different things. When a man hates, it is often characterized by sin, but since God is perfect, he cannot sin. When God hates something, it signifies a position that he has taken. In this passage, the Hebrew word for hate used literally means "to be set against." Now, if God is said to hate something, it means that he is set against it, and if God is set against something, that is serious business.

I'm sure you and I don't want to be doing something that God hates. Hence we should avoid these seven things like avoiding a deadly contagious disease. Let's discuss those seven things, after which to whatever extent we're guilty of any of them; we must confess it and ask God for forgiveness and strength to get it right.

1. A Proud Look-Is Sin

Pride can be very damaging. It is harmful to relationships. In Proverbs 13:10, it says; *"Only by pride cometh contention: but with the well-advised is wisdom."* Pride breaks up marriages, and keeps people from amending their ways with God. Psalm 10:4 says, *"The wicked, through the pride of his countenance, will not seek after God: God is not in all his thoughts."* Furthermore, pride may cause people to think they are at peace with God when they really aren't.

Proverbs 29:23 says, *"A man's pride shall bring him low: but honor shall uphold the humble in spirit."* This truth is powerfully demonstrated in Daniel, chapter 4 when King Nebuchadnezzar of Babylon amassed vast wealth and influence until his heart was lifted up with conceit. Then he dreamed a troubling dream, after which Daniel was called in to interpret the dream. Daniel relayed to him that God would bring terrible punishment upon him because of his pride, that Nebuchadnezzar would lose his mind and live like a wild beast, and that he would be returned to power after he had learned his lesson. The events happened just as Daniel interpreted and after his power had been restored, Nebuchadnezzar exclaimed in Daniel 4:37: *"Now I Nebuchadnezzar praise and extol and honor the King of heaven, all whose works are truth, and his ways judgment: and those that walk in pride he is able to abase."*

Of course, It isn't always that dramatic, but sooner or later, one way or the other, pride will ruin a person. Isaiah 2:11 declares, *"The lofty looks of man shall be humbled, and the haughtiness of men shall be bowed down, and the Lord alone shall be exalted in that day."* No wonder that Proverbs 26:12 says, *"Seest thou a man wise in his own conceit? there is more hope of a fool than of him."* In Isaiah 66:2, God said, *"...to this man will I look, even to him that is poor and of a contrite spirit, and trembleth at my word."*

When a Christian allows pride into his life, it will prevent him from being God's vessel and will ultimately cause God to chastise him. God detests a proud look. James 4:10 says, *"Humble yourselves in the sight of the Lord, and he shall lift you up."*

2. A Lying Tongue-Sin

Proverbs 12:22 says, *"Lying lips are abomination to the Lord: but they that deal truly are his delight."* Jesus said of Satan in John 8:44, *"he is a liar, and the father of it."* Which means we are in the devil's camp when we lie. God's abhorrence of lying was emphatically illustrated in the first-century church. In the early days after the events of Pentecost, members of the church in Jerusalem showed deep concern for each other. To ensure that not one of their brothers and sisters in Christ would lack, many went ahead to sell their houses and lands and brought the proceeds to the apostles to be distributed as needed. Initially, things proceeded smoothly, but whenever God begins to bless His people, Satan also tries to insert himself into the situation. Acts 5:1-5: *"But a certain man named Ananias, with Sapphira, his wife, sold a possession, and kept back part of the price, his wife also being privy to it, and brought a certain part, and laid it at the apostles' feet. But Peter said, Ananias, why hath Satan filled thine heart to lie to the Holy Ghost and to keep back part of the price of the land? Whiles it remained, was it not thine own? And after it was sold, was it not in thine own power? Why hast thou conceived this thing in thine heart? thou hast not lied unto men, but unto God. [Peter was saying, "Ananias, you have not lied to men only, but also to God."] And Ananias, hearing these words fell down, and gave up the ghost: and great fear came on all them that heard these things."*

His wife Sapphira wasn't in the room when this incident happened, but when she later came in she told the same lie as her husband was struck dead too. Verses 10-11: *"Then fell she down straightway at his feet, and yielded up the ghost: and the young men came in, and found her dead, and, carrying her forth, buried her by her husband. And great fear came upon all the church, and upon as many, as heard these things."*

The Bible doesn't tell us if Ananias and his wife were saved or if they were church members who had never been converted but what it tell us is that God completely abhors lying. He doesn't always punish the sin of lying in such a dramatic manner. If he did, I imagine there would be a lot of sudden deaths in the average church since people lie about many things other than their offerings. We can lie in many ways, and one is by making promises and commitments that we refuse to keep or by claiming to be one thing in public and being something else in private.

May God help us to understand that lying is a terrible thing to do, no matter what we're lying about, who we're lying to or where we're lying. When we lie, we can expect the consequence to come in one way or another. We should pray with Psalm 120:2: *"Deliver my soul, O Lord, from lying lips, and from a deceitful tongue."*

3. Hands That Shed Innocent Blood-Is Sin

As recorded in Exodus 20:13: *"Thou shalt not kill"* - or, literally, *"Thou shalt do no murder."* This is most importantly a warning against breaking the sixth commandment owing to the fact that God holds human life very sacred. Death is a delicate doorway through which human beings pass into one of two eternal destinies, and God alone possesses the right to open that door. This is why he has commanded, *"Thou shalt not kill."*

When we look at the medical profession's progress in saving and preserving life, we marvel. Yet, we are likewise shocked at how inconsequential life seems to be in our day. Over a dozen persons are shot or stabbed and killed every weekend in some of our big cities. Modern television, movies, music all portray images of violence and killing. Given how we watch television violence in the living room every evening, the increase in lawlessness and violence shouldn't surprise us. One of the nation's leading news outlets made a recent report that by the time they're 16, the average child would've seen 200,000 acts of violence on television. It has also been proven that children who witness violence on television grow incredibly insensitive to death. When life is being taken right in front of them, they sometimes take pictures for social media, laugh, crack jokes, and even applaud the killer. As a parent, one of the most effective steps you can take to prevent your children from getting used to such violence is to do away with the television set and the VCRs that come with it. Also, let's keep in mind that killing also involves the shedding of innocent blood in times of war. It is also murder. Just that masses are being murdered by armies instead of one person murdering another person. Bombs are dropped from airplanes, killing many who are innocent. Killing done during a war is no different from killing done by gangsters and professional gunmen. Seeing as God highly esteems human life and deeply detests human bloodshed, do we think that God will view the bloody hands of a soldier kindly on judgment day and say, "Well done, thou good and faithful servant"?

Mother Teresa, (winner of a Nobel Peace Prize) while speaking to a roomful of American political leaders, made a connection between the practice of abortion and the rising rates of violence in the streets. She said, "If we accept the policy that a mother may kill her own child, how can we tell other people not to kill each other?"

4. An Heart That Deviseth Wicked Imaginations- Sins

The Scriptures use the word "heart" to denote the whole inner person, including the feelings, affections, motives, thoughts and desires. Proverbs 4:23 says that *"out of the heart are the issues of life."* The "heart" is the center of one's physical, spiritual, and mental life.

Heart-related problems are on the rise these days. People who have high blood pressure or elevated cholesterol counts are always watching their hearts closely. But we are all battling a heart disease of a different nature. Jeremiah 17:9; *"the heart is deceitful above all things and is desperately wicked."* We must carefully watch our speech and our actions, particularly how we react to various situations that we face in life.

We are surprised with a question we would rather not answer, so instead; we try to circumvent the truth.

We're involved in a car collision, and we become upset and angry.

A colleague at work gives us a hard time, and we respond with sarcastic remarks.

These are all problems of the heart. Although we may usually be calm when things go according to plan, sudden stress signifies a heart that is not under control. Speech, actions, and habits are evident on the surface, where other people can easily observe them in our daily lives. But at sublevels lie our feelings, thoughts, desires, and motives— remaining unobserved and unknown until a time when they show themselves in speech or action.

Humans look on the outward appearance, but *"the Lord looks on the heart"* (1 Samuel 16:7). Or, according to the Psalmist, *"God knows the secrets of the heart"* (Psalm 44:21). The heart of man —in its unreformed state—is a world of evil machinations, overrun with foul imaginations and often determined to revenge. Therefore, Christians who haven't steadily rejected the imaginations woven by their carnal mind must stay alert and keep a clean house.

Heart-keeping is very similar to house-keeping. We must be consistent in sweeping out dirt and cleaning out the rubbish. Although it is the truth that we cannot prevent the devil from dropping evil thoughts into our minds, it is also true that we must not dwell upon such thoughts nor accommodate them. We are, after all, responsible for our beliefs. A statement made by Martin Luther still rings true: "You cannot stop the birds from flying over your head, but you can keep them from building a nest in your hair." It is our duty to place our thoughts into captivity and make them obedient to Christ (2 Corinthians 10:5). We must be deliberate in censoring what we read, guarding what we listen to, and being careful of the things we laugh at. God detests hearts that devise foul imaginations.

5. Feet That Be Swift in Running to Mischief- Is Sins

The dictionary defines "To run to mischief" as being eager to put something over on someone - to get by with something - to get something through deceit or trickery. Proverbs 10:23 says this about such a person: *"It is as sport to a fool to make mischief...."* And Proverbs 7:16 states: *"His mischief shall return upon his own head, and his violent dealing shall come down upon his own pate."*

Years ago, a young boy and his buddies got angry at a farmer because he forbade them from taking a short-cut through his farm. They had been climbing over his fence and trampling down his crops, and he told them not to trespass. One boy who was the ring-leader of the group slipped onto the farm one night and sowed Johnson grass over the entire farm. If you know anything about Johnson grass, you know that it spreads rapidly and takes over; it's practically impossible to get rid of. That boy grew up, fell in love with that farmer's daughter, and married her. When the farmer died, that boy inherited the farm, and he spent the rest of his life-fighting Johnson grass.

Galatians 6:7 warns, *"Be not deceived; God is not mocked: for whatever a man soweth, that shall he also reap."*

6. A False Witness That Speaketh Lies- Sins

In verse 17, He gave a general admonition against lying; but in verse 19, God makes it more specific. Here, He admonishes us in particular against lying about another person. Furthermore, the ninth commandment strictly forbids the same. Exodus 20:16; *"Thou shalt not bear false witness against thy neighbor."* The corrupt Jewish religious leaders used this approach in their efforts to condemn Jesus. Matthew 26:59; *"Now the chief priests, and elders, and all the council, sought false witnesses against Jesus, to put him to death."*

As earlier explained, we can lie in many different ways. We can lie by subtly creating false impressions, and we can lie without directly giving out wrong information or by unfairly raising questions and creating unfounded doubts about someone. We can lie by telling just a part of the whole story. Either way that we choose to lie, lying is a terrible business.

God finds it abominable, and whenever we lie, we place ourselves in a dangerous position because we will suffer the consequences without fail.

7. He That Soweth Discord Among Brethren-He Sins

God loves peace. And His first priority is that we are at peace with Him through repentance and faith in Christ. Romans 5:1-2 reads, *"Therefore being justified by faith; we have peace with God through our Lord Jesus Christ: By whom also we have access by faith into this grace wherein we stand and rejoice in the hope of the glory of God."*

The scriptures also say that Christians must do everything possible to be personally at peace with other people. Paul wrote in Romans 12:18, *"If it is possible, as much as lieth in you, live peaceably with all men."* Even more, it is our duty to encourage people around us to be at peace with God through repentance and faith in Christ and practice peace among themselves. Jesus says in Matthew 5:9, *"Blessed are the peacemakers: for they shall be called the children of God."* Obviously, the first way to be considered children of God is by receiving Christ as Lord and Savior. Still, another significant way that they can be recognized as God's children is by being committed to the job of peacemaking.

In Romans 14:19, Paul continues that theme: *"Let us, therefore, follow after the things which make for peace, and things wherewith one may edify another."* Verse 33 of that same chapter, he said, *"For God is not the author of confusion, but of peace, as in all churches of the saints."*

In Ephesians 4:1-3, Paul wrote: *"I, therefore, the prisoner of the Lord, beseech you that ye walk worthy of the vocation wherewith ye care called, with all lowliness and meekness, with long-suffering, forbearing one another in love; Endeavoring to keep the unity of the Spirit in the bond of peace."*

If a person goes about creating strife among others by whatever means, that person is in a dangerous position because God detests the person *"that soweth discord among brethren."*

So, these are the seven things that are "an abomination" to God, according to Proverbs 6:16. The word "abomination" also means "detestable, loathsome, repulsive." God hates these seven things. You may be wondering why seven? The number seven in the Bible usually denotes completeness or perfection. Hence, it tells us how thoroughly, intensely, and completely God hates those things. As earlier mentioned, the first part of verse 16 could also be translated, *"These are seven things that God is set against."* Romans 8:31 asks, *"If God be for us, who can be against us?"* But in a complete antithesis, the verses here in Proverbs 6 tell us that if God be against us, then no matter who else is for us, we're in deep trouble. The only solution in this situation is to confess our sins, and make peace with God.

All Our Righteousness are as Filthy Rags (as Sin)

Isaiah 64:6 (AMP): *For we all have become like one who is [ceremonially] unclean [like a leper], And all our deeds of righteousness are like filthy rags; We all wither and decay like a leaf, And our wickedness [our sin, our injustice, our wrongdoing], like the wind, takes us away [carrying us far from God's favor, toward destruction].*

Theologians often use this passage as proof that all the things that we think we've done right or good are actually nothing more than "filthy rags" in the sight of God. In context, this passage is referring especially to the Israelites who had strayed from God in Isaiah's time (760—670 B.C.). When Isaiah wrote it, he was concerned about his nation and their hypocrisy, but he includes himself in the description with the use of "we" and "our." Although Isaiah was redeemed and set apart as God's prophet, he considered himself part of an exceedingly sinful group. Ephesians 2:1–5 is another passage where the doctrine of total depravity is clearly taught. The example of Isaiah 64:6 could accurately be applied to the whole world, particularly with Isaiah's inclusion of himself in the description.

The word "filthy" translates to the Hebrew word iddah, with the literal meaning *"the bodily fluids from a woman's menstrual cycle."* The word "rags" *is a translation of begged, meaning "a rag or garment."* Hence, our "righteous acts" are viewed as repulsive as a soiled feminine hygiene product by God.

At the time that Isaiah wrote this, the Israelites had received countless miraculous blessings from God; still, they had disobeyed Him by making sacrifices and burning incense on strange altars (Isaiah 65:3–5), worshiping false gods (Isaiah 42:17). Isaiah had even referred to Jerusalem as a harlot and compared it to Sodom (Isaiah 3:9). These people truly believed themselves to be righteous. Yet God considered their acts of righteousness as little more than "filthy rags." Their falling away from the law of God had made all their righteous works completely unclean. *"Like the wind, [their] sins were sweeping them away"* (Isaiah 64:6). Although throughout the Bible, self-righteousness is condemned (Ezekiel 33:13; Romans 3:27; Titus 3:5), we are commanded to do good works. Martin Luther said, *"The most damnable and pernicious heresy that has ever plagued the mind of man. Is that somehow he can make himself good enough to deserve to live forever with an all-holy God?"*

Paul wrote in Ephesians 2:8–9 that there is nothing we can do to save ourselves and that our salvation is only due to God's grace. After which he proclaimed that *"we are his workmanship, created in Christ Jesus for good works, which God prepared beforehand, that we should walk in them"* (Ephesians 2:10; also look at 2 Corinthians 3:5).

We are not saved by our own efforts, personal characteristics, abilities, intelligent choices, or any acts of service that we may perform. But, as believers, we are *"created in Christ Jesus for good works"*—to help and serve others. It is the truth that nothing we can do can earn us our salvation; however, God intended that our salvation should result in acts of service. Our salvation is not only for our own benefit but for the service of Christ and the building up of the church (Ephesians 4:12). This reconciles the apparent conflict between faith and works. Our acts of righteousness do not lead to salvation but are, in fact, proof of our salvation (James 1:22; 2:14–26).

Ultimately, we must understand that even the acts of righteousness we perform are not of our own doing but as a result of God's presence within us. By our own power, our "righteousness" is merely self-righteousness and empty, hypocritical religion that creates little more than "filthy rags."

All Have Sinned (*Sin is Our Problem*)

Romans 3:23-24 [NKJV] says, *"since all have sinned and continually fall short of the glory of God, and all are justified freely by his grace through the redemption that came by Christ Jesus."*

No human being is exempted from the universal truth that all have sinned and fallen short of the glory of God. Just as we're condemned for sins of the flesh, such as murder and adultery, we are likewise condemned for our self-righteous attitudes, prideful thoughts, works of the flesh, and failure to love God with all our heart and honor Him as we should.

Deuteronomy 6:25 [NKJV] reads, *"It will be [considered] righteousness for us [that is, right standing with God] if we are careful to observe all this commandment before the Lord our God - just as He has commanded us."*

This idea is quite strange to the human heart, as we all have a tendency to whitewash our faults while enlarging our qualities, playing up our gifts, and exaggerating our graces. When Adam sinned in the garden of Eden, he sent the entire human race into the cesspit of sin. However, it should be noted that we're not condemned sinners only because of our sins; right from birth, we're born into sin and are at enmity with God. We sin because we are sinners, without any doubt. After Adam sinned, his eyes were opened, and he saw that he stood naked, impure, and ashamed before a holy God.

Sin activated the inner witness of man's conscience, which ensured that man knew the wicked and evil, but without the ability to resist it, and that he knew the good and righteous, but without the capacity to perform it. Through Adam, sin was imputed to mankind, and from our earthly parents, we inherit sin. We all commit sins because we are all sinners by birth. Therefore we are not sinners because we sin; we sin because we are sinners - born in sin. And the wages of sin for is death.

In the era of Christ, the Jews thought that their earthly lineage prevented them from partaking in the guilt and penalty of sin. Likewise, many Gentiles today believe that their morality level is enough to exclude them from any divine punishment. However, the written witness of God's perfect Law and the inner witness of man's conscience condemns the fallen sinner to death and separates sinful man from their heavenly Creator – through time and into eternity.

None of us can measure up to the glory of God. His perfect Law explains the sinless standard that He expects from humanity. Isaiah 64:6 (AMP) says, *"For we all have become like one who is [ceremonially] unclean [like a leper]. And all our deeds of righteousness are like filthy rags; We all wither and decay like a leaf, and our wickedness [our sin, our injustice, our wrongdoing], like the wind, takes us away [carrying us far from God's favor, toward destruction]."*

Because none of us can ever attain God's righteous standard, we're all left guilty, helpless, damned, and deserving of death and eternal separation from our Lord God. But He entrusted the amazing gospel of grace to the apostles and prophets, where Paul, in his epistle to the Romans, proclaims God's eternal plan of salvation with joy. *"For all have sinned and fall short of the glory of God... but they are justified freely by His grace, which is through the redemption that is in Christ Jesus."*

Chapter 2
If Sin Is Our Problem, What Gives Sin Its Power?

The Bible clarifies that *"The sting of death is sin, and the power of sin [by which it brings death] is the law."* - I Cor 15:56 (AMP)

The law and prohibitions of God are essentially what gives sin its power. It has happened to us all. We see a sign next to a river that says "Absolutely no swimming," and we immediately want to jump in and swim a lap. As children, our mothers tell us to stay out of the cookie jar, and that's when we develop the urge to have a cookie. We see a "post no bill sign" Our response is to go ahead and post one anyway. This tells you that the power of sin is in the law.

Note that this is not to say that the law is sinful. Let's see how Paul explains this in Romans 7:7-8; *"What shall we say, then? Is the law sin? Certainly not! Indeed, I would not have known what sin was except through the law. For I would not have known what coveting really was if the law had not said: "do not covet." But sin, seizing the opportunity afforded by the commandment, produced in me every kind of covetous desire. For apart from the law, sin is dead."*

The Bible goes further: *"The law came in so that the transgression (sin) would increase;"* (Rom 5:20, NASB)

The Bible says further: *"For if we could be saved by keeping the law, then there was no need for Christ to die."* (Gal 2:21)

The Ten Commandments were not given to us to stop sin. Indeed, they have no power to do so. Instead, God gave us those commandments to expose sin. Paul explains again in Romans 3:20, *"For no one can ever be made right in God's sight by doing what His law commands. For the more we know God's law, the clearer it becomes that we aren't obeying it."*

When you grasp this truth, you will get to the root of one of the church's most significant controversies today. Jesus was telling us that none of us could keep the law and that everyone requires salvation.

The law, being holy and perfect, was created to convict unbelievers of their sin and tell them of their need for the Savior. Only Jesus Christ is able to save you from the wages of sin that the law reveals. Only through Jesus Christ can you be in right standing before God.

Romans 10:4 says, *"For Christ has accomplished the whole purpose of the law. All who believe in Him are made right with God."*

Romans 6:14 shows Paul explaining further that *"Sin is no longer your master, for you are no longer subject to the law, which enslaves you to sin. Instead, you are free by God's grace."*

When Sin Is Conceived, It Gives Birth To Death

James 1:14-15 (AMP): *But each one is tempted when he is dragged away, enticed and baited [to commit sin] by his own [worldly] desire (lust, passion). Then when the illicit desire has conceived, it gives birth to sin; and when sin has run its course, it gives birth to death.*

James made it evident in verse 14 that temptation to sin always originates from within ourselves. God is never at fault. Regardless of how terrible our circumstances are, the desire to sin still comes from us. We are responsible for tempting ourselves to sin. God lets us face trials and ordeals as a way of "exercising" our faith, thereby making it more robust. It is not His will that we give up, sin, and defy Him.

James admonishes us of the consequence of falling into sin. Sin is born when we say "yes" to the desire to do what we want rather than trust God and obey Him. Sin grows up and leads to death.

Make no mistake; sin always leads to death. For unbelievers - who have not been born again to a new life - who are yet to accept God's gift of pardon for sin - that death is permanent and eternal. However, even for Christians, sin has deadly consequences. In James 5:19–20, James clarifies that when Christians successfully turn each other back from sin, they save each other from the claws of death.

Sin Is From The Devil

1 John 3:8 (AMP): *The one who practices sin [separating himself from God, and offending Him by acts of disobedience, indifference, or rebellion] is of the devil [and takes his inner character and moral values from*

him, not God]; for the devil has sinned and violated God's law from the beginning. The Son of God appeared for this purpose, to destroy the works of the devil.

The bottomless depths of Satan's habitual sin strongly contrasts with the limitless heights of Christ's eternal righteousness. From the beginning of God's revelation of Himself to mankind, the devil is seen as the despicable source of sin and scheming instigator of everything evil.

The scriptures warn us that the man or woman who sins is of the devil. He is the instigator of sin. He is the deceiver of Eve in the beautiful garden. He is the poisonous root from which all sin stems from, for Satan defied God and sinned from the beginning of time.

Whoever sins is copying Satan's actions instead of considering the goodness of God the Father. Sinners allow the destroyer of our souls to determine their actions and to turn their hearts away from the Lord. Instead of embodying the beautiful character of Christ by walking in spirit and truth and abiding in Him.

Anyone who follows Satan's practice and adopts his ways is 'of the devil'. The nature of sin, ascribed to man at the beginning, is **inextricably** linked to Satan's wicked ways. He instigated corruption and sowed deceit, and was a murderer from the beginning. He has no truth in him because he abandoned it when he disobeyed God and has proven himself to be the originator of lies.

The principle and practice of sin indeed have their roots in Satan; alternatively, divine righteousness is from the Lord Jesus. Jesus' perfect righteousness is attributed to those who are born of God. Upon salvation, the new nature given to us is Christ's own sinless nature, which cannot sin.

In contrast, the original nature we all inherited from our fallen parents can't help but sin. The old sin nature simply cannot produce any good deeds or righteous acts. We're all born sinners, but Jesus came to earth to destroy all works of Satan.

The old sin nature is of the devil, but our new, born-again nature is of God. The new Creation in Christ has been made whole, a child of the light, and has become part of God's family. And that new nature, that comes from Christ, is incapable of sinning.

For the duration of our life on earth, a believer's old sin nature is constantly waging war against our new nature and therefore needs to be kept in the place of death. But Christ came to the world in human form to pay the debt for the whole world's sin. How great is it that Christ was born into His own creation so that He might put an end to the works of the devil?

The devil has a consistently evil nature, and so he who sins is of the devil. The very nature of man is sinful, but Christ Jesus came into the world to save and rescue sinners from the clutches of Satan. By His sacrificial death and resurrection in glory, He has destroyed the works of the devil and given us victory.

Therefore let us, with a meek heart and a thankful spirit, praise our great God for His great salvation plan and tremendous hope for humanity. His plans and purposes for His children were devised to protect us from the enemy's evil plans on those who are made in God's image.

We must refrain from indulging in sin and lawlessness through our actions, words, and imaginations, and instead, we must show grateful thanks for His immeasurable mercy and amazing grace. Let us despise all that feeds the evil lusts of the devil by obediently surrendering all that we are and all that we do to His will.

The purpose of God for us is summed up in this beautiful verse; "For the Son of God came in the image of sinful flesh and suffered terrible humiliation, insults, and death, to destroy sin and sickness, destruction and death. All works of lawlessness and evil so that Christ might be all in all.

Practices of Sinful Nature

Galatians 5: 19-21 (AMP): *19 Now the practices of the sinful nature are clearly evident: they are sexual immorality, impurity, sensuality (total irresponsibility, lack of self-control), 20 idolatry, sorcery, hostility, strife, jealousy, fits of anger, disputes, dissensions, factions [that promote heresies], 21 envy, drunkenness, riotous behavior, and other things like these. I warn you beforehand, just as I did previously, that those who practice such things will not inherit the kingdom of God.*

Galatians 5:16-26 demonstrates, like no other passage, the contrast between the Spirit-filled believer's lifestyle and that of one under the control of the sinful human nature. Apart from highlighting the general differences in lifestyle by pointing out that the Spirit and the sinful nature are at war with each other, Paul also includes a specific list of the actions of the sinful nature and the fruit of the Spirit.

The sinful nature is the human nature with its corrupt desires, and it remains within children of God even after their salvation. It is their deadly enemy - Rom. 8:6; Gal. 5:17, 21. According to Gal. 5:21, people who engage in acts of sinful nature cannot inherit the kingdom of God.

Therefore, Christians must continue to resist the sinful nature and put it to death through the power of the Holy Spirit. Gal. 5:17; Rom. 8:4-14.

The acts of the sinful nature include:- Gal. 5:19-21

Sexual Immorality - any form of sexual activity or intercourse outside of the marriage union. Sexual immorality may also include taking pleasure in pornographic films, pictures or writings - Ex. 20:14; Mt. 5:31-32; 19:9; Acts 15:20, 29; 21:25; 1 Cor. 5:1.

Sensuality - that is sexuality, being a slave to one's own passions and desires till one loses all shame or sense of public decency.

Impurity - this includes sexual sins, all evil deeds and vices, and the hearts' thoughts and desires.

Idolatry - worshiping spirits, persons or graven images; placing anything or anyone above God; putting one's trust in any person, thing or institution as if they had equal or greater authority than God and His Word.

Witchcraft - worship of demons, black magic, sorcery, spiritism, and using drugs to create 'spiritual' experiences.

Hostility - deep dislike or enmity; profound, hostile intentions and actions.

Strife – altercations, animosity; a struggle for superiority.

Jealousy - resentment, envy of someone's success.

Fits of Rage - explosive anger that erupts into violent words or actions.

Disputes [that encourage heresies] - seeking power or position unrighteously.

Dissensions - disharmony; preaching decisive teachings that are against God's word.

Factions - divisions within the brethren that result into forming cliques or exclusive groups and thereby destroying the unity of the church.

Envy - resenting another person who is in possession of something that one desires.

Drunkenness - impairing one's physical or mental ability by imbibing alcoholic drink.

Riotous behavior - Inordinate feasting and festivities; a party spirit involving alcohol, drugs, sex, and such.

Apostle Paul's final thoughts on the acts of the sinful nature are severe and decisive. Paul writes in Gal. 5:21, that any so-called believer who practice these types of activities do not have eternal salvation. Rev. 21:8 and Rev. 22:15 also tells us how despicable and unacceptable such acts are. If we allow Him, the Holy Spirit is able to help us overcome.

No One Is Justified by The Law

Romans 3:20 (AMP): *For no person will be justified [freed of guilt and declared righteous] in His sight by [trying to do] the works of the Law. For through the Law we become conscious of SIN [and the recognition of SIN directs us toward repentance, but provides no remedy for SIN].*

For over two chapters, Apostle Paul has been logically laying the foundation that the whole world stands condemned before a holy God, for all have gone astray, all are guilty, deserving of death and are all in need of salvation.

Inspite of the glorious testimony of His magnificent creation and the inner witness of their own consciences, the Gentiles refused to acknowledge the Lord. Man was created with a mind to think with, free-will to help him make choices and a conscience to inform his decisions.

Also, despite having the advantage of being the vehicle through whom the Redeemer was to be born, despite being entrusted with the Scripture and despite being God's chosen witnesses on earth to spread God's blessings to all humanity, Israel, were also unable to achieve righteousness by their own human efforts.

The perfect Law was not given to make us righteous, instead it was given to produce a consciousness of our unrighteousness to God. Not to justify us but to make us aware of sin. No law or principle of law could ever make a sinner righteous. It can only highlight their desperate need for salvation.

Both Jews and Gentiles alike are equally in need of a Savior, for no one can be made righteous or justified before a holy God by his own good works or human efforts. The Law helps us to be conscious of our faults and have an understanding of the nature of sin and its grave consequences. The real function of the Law is to lead us to Christ, thereby leading us toward repentance, faith, and holy character.

Chapter 3
Christ Came To Destroy The Work Of Satan (SIN)

1 John 3: 8 (NKJV): *He who sins is of the devil, for the devil has sinned from the beginning. For this purpose the Son of God was manifested, that He might destroy the works of the devil.*

Although Christ came in all the humility and weakness of a baby, His mission was not a child's mission. John says, *"The reason the Son of God appeared was to destroy the works of the Devil".* His birth in Bethlehem invaded the Devil's territory to give us freedom from our bondage to his works and influence. Indeed, it's personal. He came to liberate you from the devil!

He came to be our salvation, but he achieved this by destroying something - the works of the Devil (SIN).

What Is The Work Of Satan?

We are excited about the Devil's works being destroyed, but what exactly are his works? 1 JOHN 3: 7 (NKJV) says, *"The work of the*

*Devil is **SINNING**."* In other words, the Devil has been Sinning since the beginning of time. He is a danger to us in so many ways, but majorly he causes havoc and sorrow in our lives through SIN and making us disobey God.

If SIN is power? Then the power needs to be rendered useless. If it is a master, we must be liberated from that master. If SIN is a work of the devil, then it must be destroyed! And this is what Christ has done.

Jesus Came To Take Away Our SINS

1 John 3:5-6 (NLT): *And you know that Jesus came to take away our **Sins**, and there is no **SIN** in him. Anyone who continues to live in him will not **SIN**. But anyone who keeps on **Sinning*** does not know him or understand who he is.

Verse 5 teaches us three important truths. The first is that Jesus appeared; earlier verses in 1 John mention that this appearance was in a real, flesh-and-blood form. Regardless of false teachers' arguments that Jesus never came as a human, believers recognize the coming of Jesus to this world (incarnation) as an essential part of the faith (John 1:1–14).

Secondly, Jesus had a specific purpose for coming to this world. He had a mission to render the power of ***Sin*** over our lives ineffective. He did this by paying the price for our sins on the cross. When Jesus made a sacrifice on the cross for humankind? He was the only one capable of delivering the full price for all sins, once and for all.

John clarifies this further in his third area of emphasis that there is no sin whatsoever in Jesus. Hebrews 4:15 echoes this teaching; *"For we do not* *have a high priest who is unable to sympathize with our weaknesses, but one who in every respect has been tempted as we are, yet without **SIN**."*

This passage is every so often construed to mean that one who **Sins** repeatedly is an unbeliever and that a believer can **SIN**, but only occasionally. Although this is possible, this passage's definitive context is focused on the results of a relationship with Christ. True fellowship with Christ cannot be characterized by **SIN** - this is part of John's response to the claim that the gospel gives people room to do wrong.

In verse 6, the general context is that a believer's life is a changed one, a believer's life will experience some level of growth (sanctification) and is expected to be considerably different from the life of an unbeliever. Of course, the degree to which a person grows in their relationship is still dependent on them, so if a believer lacks spiritual maturity, it is by no means a test of their salvation.

But those whose lives do not change - whose lives remain the same as their former life, or whose lives show no distinction between them and the unbelievers - indicates that he or she has not seen or known Jesus. Every believer is indeed a work in progress, but it is also true that every believer's life should show a significant difference when living in Christ. If a person's life offers no distinct features that separate it from that of a non-believer, there is no reason to be sure they are true believers.

THE "BLOOD" Of *JESUS* Wipes Out "ALL" Sin

1 John 1:7 (NKJV): *But if we walk in the light as He is in the light, we have fellowship with one another, and the blood of Jesus Christ his son cleanses us from all sin.*

As born-again children of God, we are enlightened by the Holy Spirit and we develop a true sight and sense of sin. After the Holy Spirit convicts us of sin, Righteousness, and judgment, we are then brought face to face with our own perversion and sinfulness.

As we become enlightened to the truth of the gospel; we begin to understand the immeasurable price that our Lord Jesus Christ paid on the Cross for us . *"for it is only by faith in the shed blood of Jesus Christ, God's only begotten Son, that we are forgiven of our trespasses and sin."* - 1 John:1:7. **His spilled Blood** has **cleansed** us from ***ALL sin.***

By Grace through ***Faith***, we have been removed from the darkness of sin and death and placed into the beautiful light of His righteousness. Our ***Faith IN JESES'S FINISHED WORK*** on the ***Cross*** has granted us access into the throne-room of ***Grace***. And if we walk in His light, we have fellowship with our heavenly Father through the Blood of Jesus His Son.

Walking with God in the light of His love helps us to become more like Him. It is not the case that He conforms into our image's likeness. Instead, we are being transformed into His image and beauty. We once walked in tune with the world, but we are no longer of the world. John asks, "what fellowship has light with darkness? *What communion can exists between a holy God and a fallen sinner?"* Salvation showed us the truth of the glorious gospel of grace, and through faith, we are called to be children of light.

Walking in the light means, living according to God's perfect life and character. We must submit to His leading and guidance by shunning evil and remaining in the realm of righteousness and truth. It is impossible for darkness to overcome the light of God because the darkness is merely the absence of God's light - the absence of God - and once in Him, darkness can never exist.

Immediately we're saved, we gain instant access into the presence of God, and when we live in the light, we are welcome to enjoy sweet fellowship with the Father. Unfortunately, when we refuse not to walk in that light, we give up that privilege. Saved but unable to fellowship with the Father.

At salvation, we not only received the forgiveness of our former sins at the Cross. We also received the ultimate cleansing of all transgression - past, present, and future - and every one of our known and unknown sins is erased by the sea of God's gracious forgetfulness.

After total forgiveness, we are fully identified with the light of God and His **Righteousness** and He makes us perfect and holy in His sight right from the first moment we believed. This cleansing flood has become ours, by faith in Jesus. <u>We Become</u> **Righteous** T<u>hrough</u> **God's** A*mazing* **Grace.**

Only the divine offering of our Lord God is adequate payment for the accumulated sin of the whole world. <u>**Only the Blood of Christ Can Cancel the Power of Sin and Satan**</u>, destruction, death, and hell itself. **Only** the powerful **BLOOD** of the **Holy Lamb** of **God** can break the chains of sin and <u>**Set the Captive Free.**</u> **Only** through "Faith" in <u>**His FINISHED Work can a Sinner be SAVED.**</u> This shows that there is indeed power in the Blood of the Lamb of God.

Following our salvation, we must desire to walk in the light as He is in the light, so that we can remain in fellowship with our Father.

If the strength of the Sin is the Law?

1 Corinthians 15:56-57 AMP

***56** The sting of death is sin, and the power of sin [by which it brings death] is the law;*

***57** but thanks be to God, who gives us the victory [as conquerors] through our Lord Jesus Christ.*

AND JESUS DEFEATED SIN BY ENDING GODS LAW.

Romans 10:3-4

3** For not knowing about God's righteousness [which is based on faith], and seeking to **Establish Their Own** [**RIGHTEOUSNESS** based on works], they did not submit to **God's RIGHTEOUSNESS. (Based on Faith in Christ)

***4** For **<u>Christ is the End of the Law</u>** [it leads to Him and its purpose is fulfilled in Him], for [granting] **RIGHTEOUSNESS** to everyone **Who Believes** [in Him as **Savior**].*

<u>WHO, WHAT AND WHERE IN THE BIBLE DOES IT SAYS JESUS HAS THE RIGHT TO CHANGE GOD'S LAW?</u>

Chapter 4
What Gives Christ The Authority to Change God's Laws?

The word of God does.

~ THE HIGH PRIESTHOOD HAS TO CHANGE FOR THE LAW TO CHANGE ~

If The Law Gives Sin Its Power (1 Cor.15:56)? HOW CAN WE Remove the LAW FOR SINS TO BE REMOVED?

~The PRIESTHOOD HAS to CHANGE FIRST!!~

~For the Word of God to CHANGE or a Law God has in place to CHANGE.~

~The PRIESTHOOD has to CHANGE FIRST!!!~

Hebrews 7: 11-12 NLT

(When the PRIESTHOOD CHANGES, the LAW must CHANGE to PERMIT IT.)

11 *So if the priesthood of Levi, on which the Law was based, could have achieved the perfection God intended, why did God need to establish a different priesthood, with a priest in the order of Melchizedek instead of the order of Levi and Aaron?*

12 *And if the PRIESTHOOD IS CHANGED, the LAW must also be CHANGE to Permit It.*

JESUS IS OUR NEW HIGH PRIEST and he Has caused the PRIESTHOOD to change.

JESUS IS OUR NEW HIGH PRIEST and he Has caused the PRIESTHOOD to change.

Hebrews 4:14-16 NKJV

(JESUS IS Our Compassionate High PRIEST)

14 *Seeing then that we have a great High Priest who has passed through the heavens, Jesus the Son of God, let us hold fast our confession.*

15 *For we do not have a High Priest who cannot sympathize with our weaknesses, but was in all points tempted as we are, yet without sin.*

16 *Let us therefore come boldly to the throne of grace, that we may obtain mercy and find grace to help in time of need.*

For a more comprehensive answer, let's look back to the time of Abraham. Abraham paid tithes to a certain priest-king (Genesis 14:18-20). The name of the priest-king was Melchizedek, the King of Salem. Salem means "Peace," so Melchizedek was the King or Prince of Peace.

However, that title also belongs to Jesus Christ. Remember this prophecy: *"For unto us a Child is born, unto us a Son is given; and the government will be upon His shoulder. And His name will be called Wonderful, Counselor, Mighty God, Everlasting Father, Prince of Peace"* (Isaiah 9:6).

To make the identity of Melchizedek more certain, see this scripture: *"For this Melchizedek, king of Salem, priest of the Most High God, who met Abraham returning from the slaughter of the kings and blessed him, to whom also Abraham gave a tenth part of all, first being translated 'king of righteousness,' and then also king of Salem, meaning 'king of peace,' without father, without mother, without genealogy, having neither beginning of days nor end of life, but made like the Son of God, remains a priest continually"* (Hebrews 7:1-3).

In summary, Melchizedek was eternal, had no beginning nor an ending of His life. Meaning He was self-existing—eternal—and could be *"a priest continually."* And He was "made like the Son of God." He was Christ.

Another attribute ascribed to Melchizedek was that He was *"king of righteousness"* (Hebrews 7:2). Righteousness is obedience to God's law, for the Bible says, *"All Your commandments are righteousness"* (Psalm 119:172). The only human being who lived a perfect life, *"without sin,"* who lived a life of righteousness was Christ (Hebrews 4:15). He is our great High Priest, as was Melchizedek (same verse).

God had placed the administration of His law in the hands of Melchizedek (Christ). But when He brought the children of Israel out of their captivity in Egypt, He placed some of that authority, like tithing, in the hands of the Levitical priesthood: *"Now consider how great this man was, to whom even the patriarch Abraham gave a tenth of the spoils. And indeed those who are of the sons of Levi, who receive the priesthood, have a commandment to receive tithes from the people according to the law, that is, from their brethren, though they have come from the loins of Abraham"* (Hebrews 7:4-5).

Hence the priestly duties, like the teaching of the law, were entrusted into the hands of the tribe of Levi. But following the death and resurrection of our Lord Jesus Christ, the priestly duties have once again been transferred back to Christ, the *"High Priest of our confession"* (Hebrews 3:1).

Today, Christ is *"a priest forever according to the order of Melchizedek"* - Hebrews 5:6

As our King of righteousness and as our High Priest, Christ is the Lawgiver. Genesis 49:10 has a prophecy that the Messiah would be a king and a *"lawgiver"* from the tribe of Judah. In James 4:12, He is also called the "one Lawgiver."

Since Christ is the divine Lawgiver, He possesses the authority to ensure that, according to His word, *"one jot or one tittle will by no means pass from the law till all is fulfilled"* (Matthew 5:18). He alone possesses the authority to make changes to God's law, and those changes are revealed in the Scriptures.

Modern religious teachers teach a heresy that he was a "law abolishes" instead of assuming His role as lawgiver. In the next installment, what He did will be explained.

Jesus Is Our Compassionate High Priest

Hebrews 4:14-16 (NKJV): *Seeing then that we have a great High Priest who has passed through the heavens, Jesus the Son of God, let us hold fast our confession. "For we do not have a High Priest who cannot sympathize with our weaknesses." But he is in all points tempted as we are, yet without sin. Let us, therefore, come boldly to the throne of grace, that we may obtain mercy and find grace to help in time of need."*

It is possible that once a politician gets elected into office, he conveniently forgets the problems of the people who elected him into office. Their interests are no longer his priority; he is only there for his own benefit. He may begin to endorse an agenda opposed to the political beliefs of those in his jurisdiction. He may block bills that would be of benefit to his constituents. His constituents may reach out to him for help, but he ignores them. Politicians are often known to lose contact with their constituents. At the point when a politician stops fighting for his people, they are hurt. They become increasingly frustrated because their needs are not being met. Ultimately, they refuse to trust, support, and vote for that particular politician anymore and replace him.

You may be feeling like this when you approach Jesus. You know he died because of you. You understand that he rose from the dead because of you and has promised to raise you too. You are confident that he entered heaven and is preparing a place for you. You know all these, but when temptation overwhelms you, you may think that Jesus is like a politician who has forgotten about his constituents. We believe that he is a great, majestic God who is far too busy with the rest of the world to bother with your little trouble. However, in Hebrews, we're told that God counters any fears you may have in going to Christ, who is your great

High Priest. He is a compassionate High Priest who understands your weaknesses and strengthens you.

In this letter, the title "Hebrews" signifies its recipients' ethnicity; "Hebrews" are Jews, but they accept Jesus as Savior and are not open to Judaism teachings. They are ethnic Jews who also follow Christ, but they still had a significant problem. In Judaism, they saw that a high priest ministered to the faithful's needs. Every year, the Jewish high priest would enter the temple at a specific time. A large, thick curtain divided the temple into two, with one side called 'The Holy Place' and the other called: 'The Most Holy Place.' The Ark of the Covenant rested Inside the Most Holy Place, and God's presence dwelt there. The high priest was the only one who could go into the Most Holy Place and approach the Ark of the Covenant. But yet, the high priest could only approach once each year after offering a sacrifice to atone for his own sins first. Some of these Jewish Christians began to wonder if Jesus could identify with their struggles and sins; after all, unlike Judaism, Christianity did not have a high priest. Could they access the same concrete comfort of peace with God through Jesus?

The world has changed from 30AD to the twenty-first century. With technology, we can travel vast distances in just days with planes, trains, and automobiles. We can receive instant information and reach other people immediately. Modern governments are democratic in nature, as opposed to a Roman Empire dictator. And so life is different and comes with different challenges.

You may wonder if Jesus can really understand what temptations feel like in the twenty-first century. Does He know how difficult it is to fight lust in this hyper-sexualized society where lewd images are used to promote clothes, relationships, and television shows? Does Jesus know how nearly impossible it is to combat sexual temptation as a teenager? Does He know how challenging it can be to obey your authorities? To respect your parents even when they offend you? To obey a government's laws that promote agendas that are not Christ-like? Does Jesus understand? Does He understand what an arduous task it is to remain firm in your Bible-based beliefs in a society that constantly demands that you compromise? Can He relate to the fact that it is politically incorrect to speak from the viewpoint of the Scripture on sexuality and marriage, raising children, abortion, and end-of-life? Has He ever experienced the struggle inside you to accept the Bible as the absolute truth when you don't know if all of it is right and true? Does He understand those struggles, or is he just like those politicians who have lost touch with their constituents?

Satan must be over-the-moon that he makes us believe that Jesus cannot relate with our temptations in the present-day. That 21st-century sins are too grievous for Him to forgive or that He is not our compassionate High Priest!

So the devil tempts us to go rely on someone else or on our own understanding, to go try another method to wipe away our sin. Seeking forgiveness in anyone else besides Jesus Christ, Our Compassionate High Priest misses on the greatest High Priest of all time.

The Old Testament had many high priests, but the Scripture never calls any of them "great." Jesus, the Son of God, is the only "great" High Priest. That is to say, Jesus is above any other high priest. He was never required to offer a sacrifice to atone for his own sins before going into the presence of God because He was in fact without sin. Jesus could enter the presence of God anytime and has even gone through the heavens, and remains in the presence of God.

Our high priest can sympathize with our weaknesses because He has been tempted in every way possible, just as we are. It doesn't matter that He was tempted two thousand years ago; sin remains sin. Whether you're disobeying your parents in 30AD or in the 21st century - rebellion remains rebellion. Denying the Word of God is the same, whether you are doing it in front of those who would prosecute you or before your friends. Jesus was tempted with the same things you're being tempted with. You can be certain Jesus was tempted to revenge against the Roman soldiers who hit Him repeatedly. Jesus definitely understood what it felt like to question the presence of God, especially in time He prayed and didn't receive the answer we would desire: "Deliverance." The Bible shows Jesus being tempted in every way, just as we are, yet he remained blameless. He gave His life so that His blameless blood atones for you, to make you "at-one" with God. Unlike a politician who forgets his constituents, Jesus Christ is Our Compassionate High Priest who sympathizes with our weaknesses as well as strengthens us in our weakness.

With this assurance, we can approach the throne of grace with confidence. Imagine standing before the throne of grace; yes, you can because Jesus is Your Compassionate High Priest. He ministers to your soul like a priest. He experiences temptation like you but never sins. He is your mediator when you stand before God. God does not deal with you as your sins deserve. Instead, he kindly deals with us because His Son paid the price of sin. Even in times that you stumble and fall, God, in His infinite mercy, wipe away your sin. Without Jesus, you do not have confidence. But with Jesus, you can approach God anytime for help.

So when faced with temptation, you should run to Jesus, Your Compassionate High Priest. He knows what it feels like to combat temptation. He knows those feelings of anger, hate, revenge, resentment, lust, greed, pride, and arrogance that you feel and also knows how to overcome them. You can't conquer temptation with your power, but you can receive strength from Him to fight by reading the Bible. Reading the Bible will help you find contentment and do away with greed. With His word, lust becomes a thing of the past. When you understand the extent of God's love for you, all hatred goes away. Ask for strength in your moments of weakness. Ask for clarity and perseverance when you're mentally exhausted—request for patience in the face of impatience. Jesus is a Compassionate High Priest who strengthens us in weakness.

Jesus has no similarities with the politician who doesn't understand your plight. Unlike the politician, he ministers to all your spiritual needs. He has remained without sin and gave his life as a sacrifice for your sin. In Him, you're confident that you can stand in God's presence forgiven. So, what do you do once you feel temptation coming up? You run to Jesus Christ, Our Compassionate High Priest.

Christ Redeem us From the Curse

Galatians 3:13 (NKJV) is a great verse that says that *"Christ has redeemed us out of the curse of the law, having become a curse for us (for it is written, Cursed is everyone hanging on a tree."*

What has Christ redeemed us from? Many Christians are familiar with redemption; we say it with all confidence that the blood of the Lamb has redeemed us. But what exactly are we saved from?

Most people would answer that He redeemed us from sin or from Satan, but in reality, Christ redeemed us from the curse of the law. Christ did not redeem us from our sins because sin is illegal and has a hold on us. The devil came in with trickery, illegally, and deceived us to fall into sin. Through this, we became sinners - something illegal and illegitimate - and for this reason, He bore our sin and terminated it on the cross.

Christ redeemed us out of the curse of the law. Gal. 3:13 explains this. According to His likeness, when God made man in His image, the plan was for man to be His representation, so God's law demands that we express and represent God.

However, man sinned and fell short of the glory of God. Indeed, man was created to express and be a representative of God, but sin made us fall short of the glory of God, and therefore, we cannot express God. Owing to the fact that we have fallen short of the glory of God, we are under a curse, and Christ came to redeem us from the curse of the law.

Humanity fell into sin, sin placed man under a curse, and the law formalized that curse.

Ultimately, when Christ came to accomplish the work of redemption, He did not come to redeem us from sin or deliver us from the power of Satan, but He came to redeem us from the curse of the law. And yes, we are delivered from sin, saved from Satan's power, but we are redeemed from the curse of the law.

By dying on the cross of Calvary, Christ perfected the extraordinary work of redeeming us from the curse of the law, to bear our sins and to lift the curse (1 Pet. 2:24).

Chapter 5
What Has Changed With The Laws Through Our New High Priest, Christ?

Christ Came To Fulfill The Law

Matthew 5:17-18 [AMP]: *"Do not think that I came to do away with or undo the Law [of Moses] or the [writings of the] Prophets; I did not come to destroy but to fulfill. For I assure you and most solemnly say to you, until heaven and earth pass away, not the smallest letter or stroke [of the pen] will pass from the Law until all things [which it foreshadows] are accomplished.*

It is a fact that Jesus usually challenged the law's interpretation and the prophets. However, He is not against or trying to destroy the Mosaic Law or the instruction given through the prophets. He set out to destroy the misuse and abuse of the law. Ultimately, Christ came to fulfill the law.

His glory shines even more clearly when we see him in his proper connection to the Old Testament. He has a relationship with all that was written.

This is not strange as he is called the Word of God incarnate (John 1:14). Reflect on these summary statements and the supporting texts.

1. The Scriptures bear witness for Christ. Moses wrote about Christ. *"You search the Scriptures because you think that in them you have eternal life; and it is they that bear witness about me... If you believed Moses, you would believe me; for he wrote of me."* - (John 5:39, 46)

2. The Scriptures are all about Christ, an implication in all the Scriptures that specifies Christ and is fulfilled only when he has come and done his work. The death and resurrection of Jesus give meaning to all the Scriptures. *"And beginning with Moses and all the Prophets, he interpreted to them in all the Scriptures the things concerning himself."* (Luke 24:27)

3. He came to fulfill all that was recorded in the Law and by the Prophets. It all pointed to him, even in places it is not specifically prophetic. He fulfilled all that the Law required. "Do not think that I have come to abolish the Law or the Prophets; I have not come to abolish them but to fulfill them. For truly, I say to you, until heaven and earth pass away, not an iota, not a dot, will pass from the Law until all is accomplished." (Matthew 5:17–18)

4. God's promises in the Old Testament are all fulfilled in Jesus Christ. This means when you are in Christ, you will have everything else that God promised through Christ. *"For all the promises of God find their Yes in him. That is why it is through him that we utter our Amen to God for his glory."* - (2 Corinthians 1:20)

5. Jesus Christ kept the law perfectly. He suffered all the consequences of sin. Therefore, the law is no longer the path to righteousness; Jesus

Christ is. The law ultimately wants to make us look to Christ for our righteousness, not law-keeping. *"For Christ is the end of the law for righteousness to everyone who believes."* (Romans 10:4)

Hence, with the coming of Christ, almost everything has changed:

1. The blood sacrifices came to an end since Christ accomplished all that they were meant to do. Jesus was the final, everlasting sacrifice for sins. Hebrews 9:12, "He entered once for all into the holy places, not by means of the blood of goats and calves but by means of his own blood, thus securing an eternal redemption."

2. The end of the priesthood stood between worshippers and God. Hebrews 7:23–24, *"The former priests were many in number, because they were prevented by death from continuing in office, but he holds his priesthood permanently, because he continues forever."*

3. The physical temple was no longer the geographic place of worship. Upon His coming, Christ himself became the place of worship. He is the "temple," the "mountain," and the "place" where we meet God. There is no geographic center in Christianity, no Jerusalem. John 4:21, 23, *"Jesus said to her, 'Woman, believe me, the hour is coming when neither on this mountain nor in Jerusalem will you worship the Father... But the hour is coming, and is now here, when the true worshipers will worship the Father in spirit and truth.'"* John 2:19, 21, *"'Destroy this temple, and in three days I will raise it up.' . . . He [Jesus] was speaking about the temple of his body."* Matthew 18:20, *"For where two or three are gathered in my [Jesus's] name, there am I among them."*

4. Christ fulfilled and ended the food laws that set Israel apart from other nations. Mark 7:18–19, *"[Jesus] said to them, ... "Do you not see*

that whatever goes into a person from outside cannot defile him?' . . . (Thus, he declared all foods clean.)"

5. Christ has put an end to civil law establishment due to one's ethnic roots. The term God's people is no longer limited to a single ethnic group or a nation-state. God's people are now exiles and visitors among all ethnic groups and all nations. Now, the will of God for states is not directly. It was inferred from the theocratic order of the Old Testament but shall now be re-established from time to time, place to place, and by means that are in tune with God's sovereign rule over all nations, and that align with the fact that faithful obedience cannot be forced by law. Therefore the state is established in God's will but is not directly ruled by God. Romans 13:1, *"Let every person be subject to the governing authorities. For there is no authority except from God, and those that exist have been instituted by God."* John 18:36, *"My [Jesus's] kingdom is not of this world. If my kingdom were of this world, my servants would have been fighting."*

Christ Fulfilled Righteousness Of Law

Romans 8:3-4 [AMP]: *For what the Law could not do [that is, overcome sin and remove its penalty, its power] being weakened by the flesh [man's nature without the Holy Spirit], God did: He sent His own Son in the likeness of sinful man as an offering for sin. And He condemned sin in the flesh [subdued it and overcame it in the person of His own Son], so that the [righteous and just] requirement of the Law might be fulfilled in us who do not live our lives in the ways of the flesh [guided by worldliness and our sinful nature], but [live our lives] in the ways of the Spirit [guided by His power].*

"The righteousness of the Law" are those things that the Law has considered fair and right for a person to do, which contrasts with the "righteousness which is of the Law" in Romans 10:5, which specifically points to the fairness of character.

Paul declares in Romans 10 that if you plan to obtain justification through the Law, then you must keep all the laws. Christ is the height of the Law for this righteousness: He has the justification that the Law was given to produce.

In Romans 8, the righteousness of The Law is interpreted as the "requirement of the Law" in many translations (e.g ESV, NASB) and has to do with equity of deed - works - not equity of character - justification -. Paul relates equity of deed to mindfulness of Spirit and inequity of deed to mindfulness of Flesh. And so we have, *"Those who are in the flesh cannot please God."* (Romans 8:8) since the flesh is not and cannot be controlled by the Law of God but is, rather, an enemy (Romans 8:7).

To further understand how Jesus taught this distinction, read the sermon on the mount. *"You have heard it said Thou shalt not commit adultery (deed), but I say If you look at a woman lustfully, you have committed adultery already" (character).* Matthew 5:27-28.

Romans 8:3-4 talks about how a sinful character can never live up to what God has required in the Law. *"For what the law could not do, in that, it was weak through the flesh, God sending his own Son in the likeness of sinful flesh, and for sin, condemned sin in the flesh that the righteousness of the law might be fulfilled in us, who walk not after the flesh, but after the Spirit."*

People in Christ have the mind of Christ and the spirit of Christ and can achieve the righteousness that the Law requires through mindfulness of the Spirit. The Law states, "No adultery," and the Law's righteous requirement is a character void of lust. This is why we are in need of salvation.

Christ has set us Free From the Law of Sin and Death

Romans 8:2 (AMP): *For the law of the Spirit of life [which is] in Christ Jesus [the law of our new being] has set you free from the law of sin and of death.*

There is a condition that comes with getting freedom - in that you can only be free from the law of death and sin if you are in Christ Jesus. This topic is usually quite complicated.

Sin sets you apart from Christ. Sin takes you outside of Christ. Sin is bondage/imprisonment/enslavement. If being alive is being in Christ, then sin is death. Hence, sin is not merely a moral failure; it means that if we are sinners, we are not in Christ. We don't dwell on this point often because it offends non-Christians. If Christians say that we are free, then everyone else is a slave and will die. And everyone who dies is a slave because they are not in Christ. These two parallel lines never meet.

Here are two instances of misunderstandings that people usually have:

(a) Some people say that though they're in Christ, they're still a slave to sin, and therefore, God doesn't love them. There is no hope for them because He doesn't love them. OR

(b) I am not a Christian, I am a sinner, but God will forgive me somehow.

Both are misconceptions. In Romans 8:2, we are clearly told that anyone in Christ is free from the law of sin and death. Christians know that any freedom you think you have is no freedom at all if you are on the wrong path. We can only find true freedom in Christ. Is this you? Is your freedom in Christ, or are you looking for freedom elsewhere?

Free Of The Guilt Of Sin And Granted Eternal Life

Romans 3:24 [AMP]: *and are being justified [declared free of the guilt of sin, made acceptable to God, and granted eternal life] as a gift by His [precious, undeserved] grace, through the redemption [the payment for our sin] which is [provided] in Christ Jesus,*

I have a little bit about justification earlier and the persons that are justified. How do we receive justification? We receive justification through the free grace of God. "The grace of God" here doesn't point to the Gospel, or what some call the terms of the Gospel. Instead, it is the free love and favor of God, in its proper form in His heart, which is beautifully demonstrated when a sinner is justified before Him. We receive justification through Christ being pre-ordained as the ransom; in Christ standing as a mediator for his people, and in God freely sending Him to bring everlasting righteousness to man. When we receive justification, we have redemption in Christ. Redemption gives us deliverance from captivity to sin, Satan, and the law. As the Redeemer, Christ bore the sins of His people and took away their reproach by suffering the law's condemnation. He stood in place of His people and received punishment on their behalf so that God might justify all of them that believe. In no way objects or contradicts God's free grace since He sent His Son as a Redeemer to work out our righteousness without any cost to humanity.

No Longer Bound by Sin

1 Corinthians 15:57-58 (AMP): *57 But thanks be to God, who gives us the victory [as conquerors] through our Lord Jesus Christ. 58 Therefore, my beloved brothers and sisters, be steadfast, immovable, always excelling in the work of the Lord [always doing your best and doing more than is needed], being continually aware that your labor [even to the point of exhaustion] in the Lord is not futile nor wasted [it is never without purpose].*

Christ's whole life and ministry was a sacrifice; He left His perfection to bear our flesh and walk in the flawed path of man. He gave all of Himself to us every day of His life, then went ahead to pay for our lives with His. We've become so familiar with the Gospel that we just might devalue it if care isn't taken. We must remember that our victory is because of Jesus' sacrifice.

Not only did His sacrifice create a path to Heaven for us, it gave us a way to be joyful now. When we think about our salvation, we must remember that apart from being a ticket to Heaven, He has also given us power over sin. We are no longer caged and bound to our flesh, and we are free! We have His Word to teach us how to overcome sin. Hide His Word in your heart. Let it fill up your mind and flow from your mouth. Herein our power lies, in His blood and in His Word.

Glory to God that we are free from sin. God could have saved us through another means that didn't involve giving up His only son, but He did it because the most meaningful gifts and freedoms are ones born through sacrifice, blood, and at high personal cost. Not monetary cost, but the cost of pain, blood, tears, humility, and service.

Chapter 6
Righteousness Completed For Us By God

Romans 10:3- 4 (AMP): *For not knowing about God's Righteousness [which is based on faith], and seeking to establish their own [righteousness based on works], they did not submit to God's righteousness. For Christ is the end of the law [it leads to Him, and its purpose is fulfilled in Him], for [granting] righteousness to everyone who believes [in Him as Savior].*

The Jews had a fervor for the Lord and were passionate about the Law because they wanted to attain the heigh of what they considered righteous. However, their righteousness was completely different from the flawless, godly righteousness that the Lord expects of His children.

The Law was given to expose unrighteousness and to cause a sinner to repent before a holy God. But the Scriptures classifies two types of righteousness; one derives from a works-based morality, achieved by laboriously keeping the Law, while the other righteousness is based on faith, which stems from humbly trusting Jesus as the Saviour and always depending on Him for help.

The Law cannot produce righteousness. Instead, it reveals unrighteousness and brings us to repentance. The Law directs us to Christ, the truly righteous one and the only One Who can ever make us as righteous as God wants. The Law can't impart righteousness to fallen man, for we are condemned when we break the law, and the wages of sin is death. Because Christ was devoid of sin, He was qualified to save us through His sacrificial death.

Christ has become the end of the Law for righteousness seeing as He suffered the punishment we deserve. Mankind is simply incapable of being righteous as required by God, but as the religious Jews of old who burned for the Lord, there are modern Christians who strive to be righteous by their own works. They spend all their time and energy on works-based righteousness, which is determined by their deeds for God, instead of what He has done for us on the cross of Calvary.

We must refrain from blindly clinging to our own works-based righteousness, while expecting that God will accept us for our good works. We are no longer in the era when God no longer deals with His people through the Mosaic Law. He now relates with us through Christ, Who became sin for us, so that we might become the righteousness of God.

Righteousness of God Apart From The Law

After seeing the righteousness of God and the righteousness that the Lord Jesus has accomplished, Romans 3:19-26 (AMP) is wonderful. Verse 19 reads, *" Now we know that whatever things the law says, it speaks to those who are under the law, that every mouth may be stopped and all the world may fall under the judgment of God."* Why did God give man the law? God gave us the law so that man would have nothing to justify himself before God, to that everyone has sinned and that everyone is a sinner. Verse 20 reads, *" Because out of the works of the law no flesh shall be justified before Him; for through the law is the clear knowledge of sin."* God's law's highest purpose was to show man that he is a sinner, not for man to be saved through it. The law is not man's saving grace; it is completely condemnatory. The law says that man should die and perish, and if that was the end of the matter, there would be no gospel. But God knew that man could not live by the law, so he devised other ways to save us. In verse 21, the first two words introduce a marvelous turn, "But now. *" But now, apart from the law, the righteousness of God has been manifested."* God's righteousness was initially manifested in the law, but if that were still the case, there would be no hope for us. What does God's righteousness was manifested in the law mean? This means that you had to pay back all by yourself if you owed God something. If you sinned, you had to perish. In this way, the law would manifest God's righteousness. After all punishing sinners would be the most righteous thing for God to do. Hallelujah! For the Righteousness of God is no longer manifested in the law. The righteousness of God is now manifested apart from the law. The end of verse 21 says, *"Witness being borne to it by the Law and the Prophets."* Even the prophets in the Old Testaments testified to the same thing.

Now, how is God's righteousness manifested? In Verse 22; *" Even the righteousness of God through the faith of Jesus Christ to all those who believe, for there is no distinction."* "Since all have sinned and fall short of the glory of God" (verse 23), how can we obtain God's grace? Verses 24 and 25 states that we are *" justified freely...thr*ough the redemption which is in Christ Jesus; whom God set forth as a propitiation place.» God has sent Jesus as our redeemer and has set Him forth as a propitiation place. In the Old Testament tabernacle, the propitiation place is the covering of the ark, the only place devoid of sin; it was the place where God bestowed grace upon man. By His blood, God has made Jesus the propitiation place, and through that blood, man can come by faith to God. Today, we have salvation because God ignored our sins but because He has dealt with them. God doesn't see us as forgiven debtors but paid-up debtors who are forgiven.

Many Would Be Made Righteous Through Christ

Romans 5:17- 19 AMP: *For if by the trespass of the one (pp0⁰Adam), death reigned through the one (Adam), much more surely will those who receive the abundance of grace and the free gift of righteousness reign in [eternal] life through the One, Jesus Christ. 18 So then as through one trespass [Adam's sin] there resulted in condemnation for all men, even so through one act of righteousness there resulted in the justification of life to all men. 19 For just as through one man's disobedience [his failure to hear, his carelessness] the many were made sinners, so through the obedience of the one Man, the many will be made righteous and acceptable to God and brought into right standing with Him.*

There are many misconceptions around the effects of sin as inherited from Adam. While it is true that we sin on an individual basis, the effects of Adam's transgressions were much more disastrous. Paul clearly teaches in this chapter that even though we sin on an individual basis, more accurately, our sin is continuous because Adam's trespass made all mankind sinners. Basically, through Adam, we inherited a sinful nature.

It is not enough to try to live a good life; try to obey all the ten commandments. We cannot break free from our sinful nature on our own accord. For this reason, Jesus said to Nicodemus in John 3, *"I tell you the truth, no one can see the kingdom of God unless he is born again."* This seems impossible to grasp until you understand the sin nature. We were born with the spirit of this world, corrupted by a sinful nature because of Adam's sin. But, 2 Corinthians 5:17 says, *"Therefore, if anyone is in Christ, he is a new creation; the old has gone, the new has come!"* This means that when you accept Jesus as your Lord and Savior and abandon all thoughts of self-righteousness outside of Christ. You are born again. We don't realize it, but a miracle occurs at this time. God removes the sin nature from you and puts His Spirit inside you. Goodbye to the old, welcome to the new. *"Who hath delivered us from the power of darkness, and hath translated us into the kingdom of his dear Son."* (Colossians 1:13 KJV). The moment you trust Jesus as your Savior, you're free of the sin nature and born again.

Adam's transgression also made it impossible for us to achieve reconciliation with God on our own accord. Through Adam, Sin brought death, but life through Jesus brought justification. Apostle Paul emphasizes that the grace we received was much more in every way. The work of Jesus completely undid what was done through Adam. Through faith in Jesus, the sin nature has been completely destroyed and removed. The abundant grace of God conquered completely.

The next thing that Jesus totally erased was guilt and condemnation as a result of our old sin nature. The gift of grace that we received through Jesus entirely destroyed sin and its effects upon our person. Suppose under the judgment of sin; we are fully aware that we're completely condemned of sin, then through Jesus. In that case, we should be fully aware that we have forgiven, righteousness, and are a holy consecrated people. *"No longer suffering under the spirit of this world, but rejoicing through the spirit of the kingdom of light through whom we have received reconciliation"* (Romans 5:11).

Grace Reign Through Righteousness Through Christ

Romans 5:20- 21 AMP: *20 "But the Law came to increase and expand [the awareness of] the trespass [by defining and unmasking sin]. But where sin increased, [God's remarkable, gracious gift of] grace [His unmerited favor] has surpassed it and increased all the more, 21 so that, as sin reigned in death, so also grace would reign through righteousness which brings eternal life through Jesus Christ our Lord."*

There are tons of Christians out who misunderstand grace. One major cause of this is that law is our native language. We speak it fluently. Humans have a native tendency to lean toward self-righteousness, dead external works, and punitive justice. Although the law should condemn us, we believe that we are capable of fulfilling the demands of the law. We do not resort outrightly to the law for justification, but we imagine that we could actually attain perfection. We even say, *"always strive for perfection."* But isn't that the law still guiding us? Naturally, as we advance in wisdom, we should grow less confident that we can ever attain perfection. Instead, we become even more confident and committed to achieving perfection because the law is our native language, not grace.

We misunderstand grace by insisting that grace is more significant than sin and then thinking that "grace" is a license to sin even more. Luckily Paul had encountered similar problems during his ministry and had foreseen those objections in Romans 6:1, where he asks, *"What shall we say, then? Shall we go on sinning so that grace may increase?"* And in verse 15, he asks, *"What then? Shall we sin because we are not under law but under grace?"* Having had the foresight of the misunderstandings, Paul went on to reply to his own questions with a stern, *"By no means!" "By no means!"*

Why is grace not a license and enticement to sin? Paul provided a longer argument for this in chapter 6. But for this section, let's see something he says at the end of chapter 5. *"grace increased all the more, so that, just as sin reigned in death, so also grace might reign through righteousness to bring eternal life through Jesus Christ our Lord."*

This makes it as though sin and grace are two warring factions battling for supremacy.

Another problem with how we discuss grace is that understand grace's victory over sin, saving grace. But we speak little of "reigning grace."

Because of God's victory over sin, we believe we are "under grace." Paul explains in chapter 6 what it means to be under grace. It means being ruled by grace. Grace reigns over us. "Sin shall not be your master, because you are not under law, but under grace" (6:14). If sin shall not be our master because grace masters us, then grace reigns. It rules.

How then does grace reign in the Christian life? Through righteousness. When grace conquers sin, it establishes the reign of Righteousness until eternal life is consummated. And for this reason, grace and license contradict. License reigns over a life filled with lust and sin and death, but once we've been freed from that, we're dead to the law and to sin. Each day we should *"count ourselves dead to sin, but alive to God in Christ Jesus"* (6:11). If at the start of your day each day, you deem yourself dead to sin but alive to God in Christ Jesus, you no longer allow sin to reign in your body by listening to its evil desires (6:12). Grace and license contradict because grace reigns through righteousness.

This is almost certainly where we jumble it up the most. Maybe that's why it seems to us that invoking grace is like tempting sin. Christians often leave an unrepentant sinner in their sins by saying things like "leave them. It's all about grace anyway." Why does this sound like the seasoned unbeliever who says God must forgive him his sins because "that's what God does anyway?"

If Paul heard us thinking of grace in these terms, he might say something like, *"Absolutely not! By no means!"*

Many of these statements somehow separate the idea of grace from righteousness. *"For the grace of God has appeared that offers salvation to all people. It teaches us to say "No" to ungodliness and worldly passions, and to live self-controlled, upright, and godly lives in this present age, while we wait for the blessed hope—the appearing of the glory of our great God and Savior, Jesus Christ, who gave himself for us to redeem us from all wickedness and to purify for himself a people that are his very own, eager to do what is good." (*Titus 2:11-14). Grace teaches us to "just say 'no'." Grace instructs us in righteousness. Grace becomes a cleansing agency for us and makes us want to do good. Grace reigns in the life of the Christian by inculcating and cultivating righteousness.

We must beware of godless teaching that *"changes the grace of our God into a license for immorality and deny Jesus Christ our only Sovereign and Lord"* (Jude 4b). And we must also be mindful of our heart's tendency to turn grace into lawlessness. Or to rely on the law as a means to achieve righteousness. Both contradict the gospel. God's true grace transforms the lawless into the righteous and gives eternal life where the law gives death.

Chapter 7
It Is Finished

John 19:30 [AMP]: *30 When Jesus had received the sour wine, He said, "It Is Finished!" And He bowed His head and [voluntarily] gave up His spirit.*

"It is finished." "It is done..." These are the last six words the Lord uttered from the cross.

The statement "IT IS FINISHED" can mean defeat; it can mean despair, a crushing sense of failure, or unwilling surrender. It can stamp the end of a career, marriage, or vision. Many people utter these words in a tone of defeat, to mean that their life is finished, done, or over.

To some, Christ's last words from the cross sound like "I give up." But The Messiah did not give up. He said, with complete confidence: {Jn 10:18, NLT} *"No one can take my life from me. I lay down my life voluntarily."*

The statement "IT IS FINISHED" can also be an expression of sheer relief. The relief that accompanies certainty after uncertainty is the end of a difficult task after a series of failures or a well-deserved rest after an arduous assignment.

For instance, during the Thanksgiving holiday, when you've been cooking all day, and after you take out the turkey from the oven, you say, "it is finished."

To another set of people, the six words of Christ means, "At least that's over." Of course, he was relieved that his suffering was over, but it was apparent that Christ had a strong resolve as is clearly illustrated in Gethsemane where his soul was *"crushed with grief" and still he prayed three times, "Not as I will, but as you will."* Mt 26:38, NLT.

And at other times, "It Is Finished" is a statement of great triumph. A shout of victory and fulfillment of an assignment. It can also mark the start of a new life, fresh opportunities, or bigger dreams.

Death in Adam or Life in Christ?

Romans 5:15: *"But the free gift is not like the transgression. For if by the transgression of the one the many died, much more did the grace of God and the gift by the grace of the one Man, Jesus Christ, abound to the many."*

Paul contrasts Adam's sin's disastrous effects on many with the wondrous effects of God's gift and grace, which abounds to many. Adam's sin has a devastating impact on many, meaning the entire human race. Sort of like a ripple effect, only one man sinned, but many died. On the other hand, many cannot refer to the entire human race, only to those who *"receive the abundance of grace and the gift of righteousness"*

(Romans 5:17). It would be a mistake to think that the second "many" means that salvation is offered to everyone because, in Romans 5:16, the second group is indeed justified. Instead, it means the many who truly receive the gift of eternal life through Jesus Christ.

Paul makes use of words like "grace," "gift," and "abound" in the passage to help us realize the wonder of God's gift of salvation provided free of charge to us at the expense of Christ. This undeserved gift abounds to us by the grace of God and the grace of Christ, who are connected in this verse. No matter how much sin you've accumulated, the grace of God in Christ Jesus is more abundant. Are your guilt and debt great? The free gift and abounding grace of God is greater!

Christ's work is greater than Adam's sin because it subdued many sins to bestow justification freely Romans 5:16: *"The gift is not like that which came through the one who sinned; for on the one hand the judgment arose from one transgression resulting in condemnation, but on the other hand the free gift arose from many transgressions resulting in justification."*

Adam's sin lit the forest fire that destroyed the human race, but Christ quenched the fire and then planted a new, everlasting forest for everyone who will receive His free gift.

The significant difference here is that one sin led to the reproach of the whole human race, yet the numerous sins of that condemned race gave rise to the justification for all believers. "Believe" here is implicit, not stated because from Romans 3:24-51, Paul insisted that justification is only received by faith. The work of Christ causes those who benefit from it to reign in life Romans 5:17: *"For if by the transgression of the one, death reigned through the one, much more those who receive the abundance of grace and of the gift of righteousness will reign in life through the One, Jesus Christ."*

How can we escape the devastating reign of death? Through Jesus Christ, by receiving "the abundance of grace" and "the gift of righteousness." Paul again points to the abundance of grace to teach us that there is no chance whatsoever of God's gift finishing before it reaches you. The gift of Christ's righteousness, or justification. Not only does he forgive your sins; He also gifts you the positive righteousness of Christ so that when you stand before God, you stand not in your own righteous deeds but in the righteousness of Jesus Christ.

In summary: We were all condemned through Adam's sin, but those in Him are justified through Christ's righteousness.

Romans 5:18-19: *"So then as through one transgression there resulted in condemnation to all men, even so through one act of righteousness there resulted in the justification of life to all men. For as through the one man's disobedience, the many were made sinners, even so through the obedience of the One the many will be made righteous."*

Verse 18 is a completion of the idea that Apostle Paul began in verse 12: that one man's sin caused death and condemnation to all, but One Man's righteousness gave justification of life to all. Note that Paul's teaching is not on universalism -that all people will be saved- as that would contrast with where he teaches that sinners will be judged and eternally condemned (2:5, 8, 9). Furthermore, he has just said in 5:17 that only those who receive the gift of righteousness would reign with Christ. Instead, both "alls" refer to their representative heads. That is, all who are in Adam are condemned, and all who are in Christ are justified. If you recollect, the same applies to the "many" in verse 19: Through one man's transgression, the many (the human race) were made sinners, and through One Man's sacrifice at the cross, the many (believers) made righteousness.

The word "made" means to appoint, but we must interpret it here in relation to the forensic context. To be 'righteous' does not translate to moral uprightness, but to be judged innocent in the heavenly judgment.

Therefore Paul is doing a recap of 5:12-17 in verse 18 and reiterating it in language that's a bit different in verse 19. The primary focus of this is that if you are in Adam, you're under the reign of sin and headed for eternal damnation. But if you are in Christ, you are free from sin and death and will reign in life through Him, again because Christ's gift is greater than Adam's sin could ever be.

We've spent a lot of time explaining these difficult verses, but let's sum it up by paraphrasing some of the practical applications:

- Fathers, the choices you make will either positively or negatively affect your children, so be mindful and live prayerfully. Luckily, our sins won't have the ripple effect that Adam did, but nevertheless, we don't sin in isolation. Consider how your choices will influence your children.

- The human race has a universal problem of sin, and so it only fits that the versatile solution is the gospel. From the most primitive tribes to the most sophisticated professors, the problem and the solution remain the same. Don't let someone's Ph.D. intimidate you. He is a sinner and he needs Christ. Point him to Christ.

- If the human race is plagued by the guilt of identifying with Adam's sin, then we cannot receive salvation through adding our good deeds. To receive God's gift through Christ, we must be identified with Christ's righteousness by faith.
- Anyone who is in Christ has secure salvation, not because of anything they did, but because they abide in Him. You are saved by Christ's obedience on the cross and by putting your sole trust in Him. Where are you? In Adam, controlled by the reign of death? Or, are you in Christ by faith, reigning in life?

Christ Makes Us Right With God By Faith

Romans 3:22-26 NLT: *We are made right with God by placing our faith in Jesus Christ. And this is true for everyone who believes, no matter who we are. For everyone has sinned, we all fall short of God's glorious standard. Yet God, in his grace, freely makes us right in his sight. Through Christ Jesus, he did this when he freed us from the penalty for our sins, for God presented Jesus as the sacrifice for sin. People are made right with God when they believe that Jesus sacrificed his life, shedding his blood. This sacrifice shows that God was fair when he held back and did not punish those who sinned in times past, for he was looking ahead and including them in what he would do in this present time. God did this to demonstrate his righteousness, for he himself is fair and just, and he makes sinners right in his sight when they believe in Jesus.*

Humans' sinful nature is in stark contrast with the endless righteousness of the everlasting God. The depravities of humanity are explicitly illustrated in the first three chapters of Romans. Paul makes it crystal clear that no one is righteous and no one is exempt from condemnation and the wrath of God.

Before the coming of Christ, the Law determined righteousness. However, due to humans' sinful nature, the standard of righteousness required by the Law is unattainable. Romans 3:21 begins to reveal righteousness different from the Law's - the righteousness of God.

Paul begins to explain how a man can attain God's righteousness but only by being declared righteous by God and then God's own perfect righteousness be ascribed to him. But God's righteousness is only received by grace through faith in the death, burial and resurrection of the Son, for the forgiveness of sins and eternal life. The Law was merely a tool to reveal men's sinful nature. Prophets of old testified to this fact by reminding us that the just will live by faith and not by the works of the Law. The Word of God stands witness to the fact that God's righteousness is only attributed to man by faith and not by works, nationality, parentage, race, color, age, or sex.

Apostle Paul wants to let us know that asides from the law's unattainable Righteousness, God's Righteousness is attainable to all. but can only be obtained by having faith in Jesus Christ. The Righteousness of God is imputed to anyone who believes in Him, without distinction and regardless of race, age, sex, etc.

Thanks be to God that despite our sins, He sent His Son to die for us and declare us Righteous in Him - not by works of the Law but by the righteousness of God through faith in Jesus Christ our Lord and Savior who came to be the perfect Son of Man and the perfect sacrifice for the sin of the entire human race.

Some people don't think His last words on the cross sounds anything like a cry of triumph, but when He prophesied at His own death, He said in John 27, "It was for this very reason I came to this hour." For Jesus,

"**IT IS FINISHED**" was a straightforward victory declaration. A way of saying that he had fulfilled His purpose and completed His mission. What mission DID Christ accomplish? What purpose did He fulfill? What task did he complete?

- **Jesus gave His life to atone for our sin, shoulder our guilt and pay the price for our transgressions**. **John 1:29***: "[Behold], the Lamb of God who takes away the sin of the world!" And First John 2:2: "He is the atoning sacrifice for our sins, and not only for ours but also for the sins of the whole world."*

- **Jesus gave His life to redeem us from slavery and sin. Matthew 20:28:** *"the Son of Man [came] ... to give his life as a ransom for many."*

- **Jesus gave His life to reconcile us to God.** **Romans 5:10:** *"When we were God's enemies, we were reconciled to him through the death of his Son."*

- **Jesus gave His life to include us Gentiles who trust in him in the covenant**. **Ephesians 2:13:** *"now in Christ Jesus you who once were far away have been brought near through the blood of Christ."*

- **Jesus gave His life to subjugate Satan and death**. **Hebrews 2:14-15:** *"he... shared in [our] humanity so that by his death he might destroy him who holds the power of death – that is, the devil – and free those who all their lives were held in slavery by their fear of death."*

- **Jesus Gave His Life So We Can Have God's Righteousness and not our own.** **Romans 10:3-4 AMP** *" For not knowing about **God's Righteousness** [which is based on faith], and* seeking to establish their own [righteousness based on works], they did not submit to **God's Righteousness**. *⁴ For Christ is the end of the law* [it leads to Him and its purpose is fulfilled in Him], for [granting] **Righteousness to everyone who believes [in Him as Savior].**

- **Jesus Gave His Life To Destroy the Works of Satan. 1 John 3:8 AMP** *"The one who* **PRACTICES SIN** *[separating himself from God, and offending Him by acts of disobedience, indifference, or rebellion] is of the devil [and takes his inner character and moral values from him, not God];* **for the devil has SINNED and violated God's law from the beginning. For this purpose, the Son of God Appeared to Destroy the Works of the Devil."**

- <u>**Jesus Gave His Life to Remove the Curses from Our Life.**</u> **Galatians 3:13 AMP** *"Christ purchased our freedom and redeemed us from the curse of the Law and its condemnation by becoming a curse for us."*

- <u>**Jesus Gave His Life So We Can by His Blood be Cleans of ALL SIN.**</u> **1 John 1:7 AMP,** *"but if we [really] walk in the Light [that is, live each and every day in conformity with the precepts of God], as He Himself is in the Light, we have [true, unbroken] fellowship with one another [He with us, and we with Him], and* **the blood of Jesus His Son Cleanses Us From All Sin [by erasing the stain of Sin, keeping us cleansed from Sin in all its forms and manifestations]."**

- <u>**Jesus Gave His Life So WE Can Be Justified with God and SAVED through CHRIST**</u> **Romans 3:24 AMP** *"²⁴ and are being justified [declared free of the guilt of sin, made acceptable to God, and granted eternal life] as a gift by His* *[precious, undeserved]* [a]*grace, through the redemption [the payment for our sin] which is [provided] in Christ Jesus,*

Through His death, when Christ Proclaimed, **"IT IS "FINISHED,"** Christ has achieved all Those Blessings ABOVE for US, and even more. Through His death, resurrection, and ascension, he has fulfilled an even higher purpose: to establish the kingdom of God and bring many sons and daughters into SALVATION **(ROMANS 3:24)** The last words from his lips, "IT IS FINISHED," translates to "Mission Accomplished!"

HALLELUJAH!! HALLELUJAH!! HALLELUJAH!!

THIS IS ALL ABOUT THE

"FINISHED WORK OF CHRIST"

HE DID IT ALL FOR YOU!!

IN THE MIGHTY NAME IN CHRIST JESUS CHRIST MIGHTY NAME WE RECEIVE IT ALL.

AMEN, AMEN, AMEN!!!

www.ingramcontent.com/pod-product-compliance
Lightning Source LLC
Chambersburg PA
CBHW071913070526
44583CB00016B/1971